Never Forgotten

—

Foreword by Dave Roever

Wade Franks
With Mark Beaird

www.xulonpress.com

To find out more about the ministry of Wade Franks go to:

www.wadefranks.org

Table of Contents

———

Foreword

This is a foreword, but for it to work, you have to look backward, and most of life cannot be spent looking backward. But those who fail to recognize history, which is looking backward, will not have a clue as to how to read the road map of the future. Wade Franks looks backward to bring to the reader today a lesson so thoroughly learned that it will be applicable in principle to the reader as much as it was to the writer. Wade is pure. I know this man personally and have enjoyed at great lengths opportunities of fellowship for days, not just during Vietnam Journey Back tours, but also while riding alongside him and his wife Gail on motorcycles to Canada, Colorado, and any place we could find to share time together. In his book, *Never Forgotten,* you will see the progression of God's grace – His covering even when we don't see His hand; the way He shapes a man. Wade did not realize those fingerprints were God's. God will use the unleashed and unrestrained, inexplicable, undaunted, enthusiastic author of this book to change your life. This book will make the hair stand up on the back of your neck, and you'll reach up to push it back down, as a shudder goes through your body that makes you want to shout. Well, go ahead! It will make this book that much more fun to read.

Dave Roever

Dedication

**To my wife Gail,
you are the most virtuous Christian woman I know.
You are God's gift to me,
and my love for you will last forever.**

Preface

For the "grunt" or the "ground-pounder" on the battlefields of Vietnam, the moon and the stars were regular reminders of home. The country in which they had found themselves was so unfamiliar in appearance, so foreign in customs and people. For most there was little to remind them of home except for the night sky. Surrounded by the darkness, quietly standing a post or lying silently in a foxhole vigilantly watching for the stealthy approach of the enemy, it was only natural to become keenly aware of one's surroundings. The smells and sounds of the jungle would grow alive with each passing hour. When the moon could be seen, it would often draw their attention upward and lead some soldiers to think of home and wonder, *Is someone back home looking at the same moon as I am? Are they thinking of me?*

Some had someone back home who was praying for them. Many knew that there was someone at home who cared. But with all that they had heard about what was happening back in the States with protestors and politicians, many wondered how much the country as a whole cared about their troubles. So lost in the immensity of the war and the landscape of world events, it was easy to wonder if anyone would ever know what they experienced if they did not make it back home, and if they did, could they ever tell anyone or make them understand?

With their upward glance to the moon, they would cast their hopes to the sky to see home again and to be remembered. While in this foreign land which seemed an immeasurable distance from home, their gaze at the moon was a search for connection with the former world and its people they had known, while in this foreign land which seemed an immeasurable distance from home.

This is one soldier's inspiring story of how his life was brought full circle from the mud and despair of the Vietnam battlefield that caused his life to go completely off course to a healing restoration and a guiding revelation of God's divine care and plan for his life.

Introduction

The Vietnamese communist soldier just stood there yelling at me—what he was saying I could not tell you—but by his tone, expressions and actions it was no doubt filled with obscenities. He had just finished his verbal assault on my wife moments before which ended in her paperwork being crumpled up in his hand, slammed onto the counter and her being sent to the end of the line of people waiting to cross into the country through customs. Now he had turned his anger and his obvious dislike for Americans on me. His demeanor and his tone told me that he wanted me to respond. He wanted me to fire back at him, but I dared not do it. I had come too far and too much was at stake. Besides, I am confident that he wanted an opportunity to use the club which hung on his belt on an American.

The verbal barrage continued as I questioned myself as to why a man would take such abuse. Why would I be trying to get back into a country that I had one time thought that I would never leave? I felt the natural impulse to respond that any man would feel. It is natural to want to push back when pushed. But more was at stake than manly pride and more at work here than a communist government. So, I endured, having resigned myself to go the distance and complete a journey that would later reveal to me greater depths and greater truths about God's ability to work in my life than I had learned thus far.

But most importantly, I would see more clearly the hand of God that had held me, guided me, and preserved me through the years. And, later, never would His voice be clearer that it was when He spoke softly—yet clearly—to me about the meaning of my journey.

The work God is doing presently in my life is a reflection of the work God has done in the past and a foretaste of what He will do in the future. This communist soldier trying to intimidate me could no more keep me from where God was taking me than he could have prevented me from arriving at this point in my life. I had yielded myself to a greater power than he possessed and to a greater purpose than he could understand. *Let him yell*, I thought. All I have to do is not respond to this battle in the natural—God would fight this battle for me and I would be victorious!

The slamming of the soldier's stamp on my passport brought me back to the moment at hand. It was over. The soldier had to do what he hated the idea of doing. He had to step aside and yield the way. As simple as that, I was back in the country that had become so much a part of me.

CHAPTER 1

In the Nam

Only nineteen years old, I was fresh from my rural home in northern Alabama when I found myself at the beginning of a journey of a lifetime. It was 1968, and I was a soldier fighting for my country and for the country of South Vietnam which was being threatened by the Communist country of North Vietnam. All that was Vietnam was alien to me. Being on the other side of the world from my home and what would happen to me there over the next eighteen months could not have been conceived by my mind prior to arriving in this foreign land and being caught up in war. To say that I felt hopeless was an understatement of my emotional condition.

I will never forget the day the severity and hopelessness of my circumstance came crashing down on me as the never-ending fear wore away at me. I had been in Vietnam for only two or three months and I had already seen so many good men die around me that it had left me with the unmistakable feeling that I would soon be next. It was a common feeling. In fact, those of us in my squad would often sit around and speculate that maybe this would be the day that it would happen. Maybe this would be the day we would die. Maybe we would get hit in the arm or the leg, and it would be a wound that would send us home—anything but getting it in the head. We had seen it before. No one wanted to be shot in the head.

Wade in Vietnam, 1969

In one of the first firefights that I would experience, I made it through unscathed but clearly shaken from the ordeal. The fear I experienced in those early battles as I heard the popping sound of an AK-47 was overwhelming. One minute we would be moving along on patrol and the next we were embattled with the enemy in a deafening exchange of gunfire. With multiple M-16s and AK-47s firing at once in close range, nothing could be heard over the loud exchange. This made it all the more confusing because calling to one another was almost useless until the exchange subsided. At night it was even worse. I would be surrounded by the muzzle flashes of both sides, making it impossible to see everything.

A similar firefight had just ended, the enemy had disengaged, and we started out again on the move to our destination. I remember feeling an uncomfortable wetness on the back side of my hip. I slid my hand down onto my hip to attempt to identify the source of this uncomfortable feeling. Right away I felt what seemed to be wet, raw flesh. My legs went weak and I thought that I was going to pass out. Fear went through me as I assumed I had taken a hit during the firefight just minutes before. A soldier walking close to me saw the look on my face and asked, "Hey man, what's the matter?" I said to him, "I think I've been hit!" I was a "newbie," just arrived, and did not even know his name. Nevertheless, he had been in the "booneys" (Vietnam's remote jungles and mountains) for a while and was unshaken by my comment or concern. He stopped to check me since I could not clearly see the area and frankly was afraid to look. "Pull your pants down!" he instructed me unceremoniously. Standing there on the trail, I complied and waited for the news that I had been wounded.

"You've just got a leach on you! You ain't been hit." Twisting around, I looked to see that a large leach, about the size of my index finger, had attached itself to me and began to make a meal of my blood. The guy took a lit cigarette and burned the leach to make it turn loose. Once free of the leach, we just moved on through the jungle. It was just a scare; I had not been hit. Nevertheless, the thought of when the day would come that an enemy round would find me was a very real worry that would stay with me night and day.

Both the hopelessness of my circumstances and the ever-present fear that gripped my mind quickly began to take their toll. I remember sitting under a canopy made from my poncho during one of countless downpours thinking, *I'm going to die here and no one will ever know what happened to me or what I went through before I died.* Perhaps I would just be taken out of here in a body bag, shipped home in one of those coffins, buried and forgotten. I was simply going to fall off the face of the earth to never be heard from again. Even if by some miracle I survived, how could I ever make anyone understand what I saw, what I had felt and what I and others had been through in the jungles of Vietnam?

Why should it matter? It mattered to me because when replacements came fresh from the States, they would tell us about what was happening back home. They would tell us about how no one cared about the war and about how that the protestors even condemned the U.S. soldiers. It mattered to me that people understood that we were not just expendable and that our sacrifices—especially of those who died—were not meaningless. In my mind, those back home needed to know about what these men were doing and enduring for their country. It mattered because they mattered.

The feeling that no one cared and that no one appreciated these men was hard to bear at times. It was not like it is today when our country will support the U.S. soldiers regardless of their feelings about the war. There was a clear sense of being alienated from one's country. It was easy to see those jungles as the end of one's journey in this life. But the jungles of Vietnam were not the end of my journey. They were only the beginning. I would not die there in the mud of the A Shau Valley.

In the coming years, God would lead me on an incredible journey through events and circumstances that still seem unreal at times, and yet, they are the landmarks along the road that help me to see just how far the Lord has brought me and all that He has done in my life over the last thirty years.

It mattered little to God that I understood all that He was doing at the time or even that I understood that He was at work for my good all along. He knew the day would come that my eyes would be opened and the pieces of the puzzle would come together. So, He waited and worked as He journeyed with me.

CHAPTER 2

Hope and Hopelessness

———

In retrospect, I still find myself thinking that no one will ever really know—except for the men who served—what life in combat in the jungles of Vietnam was really like. Most Hollywood versions are inaccurate or embellished to create a story that they want people to hear. However, the hopelessness that is often portrayed or spoken of was real. Many times you would see soldiers who had been in battle over and over just sitting or standing motionless with a "far away stare" in their eyes. The "stare" revealed the emptiness some felt in their souls. The constant fear and the endless loss of life on both sides could drain a soldier of all the emotional connections he had previously known.

"It don't mean nothing!" was a common phrase that was used concerning things that once mattered or meant something. Thoughts of home, thoughts of the future, plans, dreams, they were all the same—outside our grasp. We were there in the "Nam" regardless. We were afraid to desire anything because of all that had been taken away from us. Maybe it was our youth, maybe it was innocence; maybe it was our dreams for

the future that any young man would have. I don't know, but
something inside of us had been taken and it was just gone.

Wade with his M-60

For me, my youth was slipping away from me quickly.
My world had radically changed in a matter of months and
all that was familiar was gone. Now my world consisted of
life in the "booneys" and the friends that I had made in my
company. The "booneys" were the remote areas of Vietnam
which, aside from being isolated from cities and towns,
consisted of jungles covering rough mountain terrain where
the hillsides and valleys were matted with thick undergrowth
and thorny vines. For my company, B/2/501st of the 101st
Airborne, our "booneys" were called the A Shau Valley.

The 101st Airborne consisted of some of America's finest young men from various backgrounds from all over the United States. Though young men, they held their own with a battle-hardened enemy. The North Vietnamese Army (NVA) had been hardened through many years of battle and most likely was made up of North Vietnamese and Chinese regular army.

But our boys never wavered in their duty. Though the politics governing the war and even the objectives of the war changed, these young soldiers sought to do their duty. Whether they understood everything about the ultimate plan or not, one thing was always clear. They were fighting for one another and fighting to get back home.

The Bond of Soldiers

There is something about the bond forged between men who have endured the heat of battle and felt the incredible fatigue that threatens to drain one's last ounce of energy. These men have felt the loss of friends and comrades in arms and have known the desperate hopelessness of looking into a future with a greater promise of death than of life.

Perhaps this is why war stories told by men who really were not there instantly ring hollow in the ears of those who have borne the burden of battle.

Looking back, I also remember the Vietnamese people that we encountered on patrol. I really did not dislike the people of Vietnam that I encountered. In fact, I felt sorry for them. I was never able to get to know any of the people like soldiers stationed near the cities. My company was never stationed near any of the larger cities or towns so I do not share the same experiences that others had that were. For me the setting was always in the booneys, the jungle and the remote mountain areas—except for the times I had limited R and R or when I had been wounded and had been medivacked to a hospital.

Nevertheless, I imagine that the people viewed me and the other American soldiers with suspicion. *What were these Americans going to do? Will they take over our country as others have tried to do in the past?* They surely wondered what would happen to them and what our ultimate plan would be for them. Little did they know all we wanted was to go home.

Life in the Booneys

Night was the worst time in the booneys. The NVA would often do their deadliest work under the cover of darkness—especially during rainy or foggy weather. Any time inclement weather would set in, the NVA would use it to their advantage. When it rained we knew that it was likely that we would be attacked—and it rained most nights. Rain and darkness almost always meant that we would be encountering the NVA. The mountain tops of the A Shau Valley would be covered with thick fog or clouds when the weather turned damp. Those were the ridges on which we traveled so we were rarely dry for any length of time.

The reason for using the cover of the rain and fog was that they were well aware of the fact that in such cases the weather would make it impossible for us to call in air support of any kind. They knew that we depended on the jets and the Cobra gunships. But in the dense fog, the jets could not see where we were and the helicopter gunships were no better off. We would be on our own without reinforcements until the weather broke. In these situations, it was just the NVA and us, and they had the upper hand.

Consequently, this is when they would be on the move. Perhaps this is why we were never able to completely shut down the Ho Chi Minh Trail. They could always find a time and a way to keep things moving. After all, this was their country and they were familiar with everything about it—

from the terrain to the weather—and how to make it work
for them. As we would say, they had the "home court advantage," and they used it.

The terrain was rough where we were. Up and down the
ridges we would go carrying fifty to seventy pounds on our
back with food rations, ammunition, and water, constantly
alert to any movement or anything out of the ordinary. It
was tough going and a hard existence. Most of us were eighteen to twenty-two years old. Sometimes our commanding
officers (CO) would be only twenty-five or twenty-six. We
traveled in squads. A "squad" was usually made up of ten
to twelve men—it varied but was usually about a third of a
platoon. This was our family in the booneys.

Wade, Drake and Stewart

Though we were young, we were constantly tired—
worn out to the point of exhaustion. I have seen days when

we were so deep under the mountain canopy of trees, vines and vegetation that I wondered if anyone knew where we were. The sound of a chopper overhead would ease my feelings of isolation because when I heard that sound overhead I at least knew that help could come. Even if we could not see them, maybe they knew where we were and could still get to us.

What we looked forward to were simple things. It was a luxury if we had a B-2 unit and canned peaches and pound cake. Hickory smoked cheese in a can, good cool water, fresh c-rations, clean socks, letters from home and such dropped to us from a helicopter were enough to refresh us.

It's odd what I thought about when I was in the field and having those doubts that I would ever get home again. For instance, I never thought that I would smell freshly cooked cornbread again—that's important to an Alabama boy. I also never thought I would sleep between clean sheets or ever have a wife and a family. The future was intangible and far too distant to grasp or to hope for in the world in which I was entangled.

Letters from home were great. In our squad, we would often find ourselves sitting and talking about our families and our homes. It was hard to think of things so far from us and from our reach, but at least it was something good to talk about. Those talks were where we really got to know one another.

There were men like Douglas Wineglass, a strong, stout black guy who was soft-spoken and often altogether quiet. He was from Monk's Corner, South Carolina, and he was my buddy. I remember him as a dependable and solid soldier. One odd thing that comes to mind was how much body heat he could produce. We often had to sleep back to back, sometimes while sitting up in order to stay out of the mud. It did not matter how much it rained or how damp those mountains got, Wineglass was warm — so I stayed close to him when we got a chance to stop and rest.

Wade and Don Stewart

Robert Watt was only eighteen years old, the youngest in our squad, and straight from Humble, Texas. He was probably one of the bravest and best all-around soldiers that I saw in Vietnam. He was always ready to walk point and often volunteered for difficult assignments. Watt was a great guy. In my mind I can still see him. A lean dark-haired young man, he was not always the neatest soldier in appearance. No one really cared about their appearance in the booneys, but Watt would often end up with a uniform a size or two too large. But he didn't care. I see him standing there with the side pockets of those baggy pants stuffed to capacity. His pockets were always packed with something. He was a true soldier.

There was our Commanding Officer, a West Point graduate, Captain Kurt Franzinger. He was from West Virginia and a man that I greatly admired. Captain Franzinger was the kind of CO that really cared about his men and always had an encouraging word for us when the times were tough. Though he was only twenty-five or twenty-six, he had the ability to lead men and was destined for great things.

Our platoon sergeant was Dave Testerman from Michigan. He had been in Vietnam a few more months than I had. Sergeant Testerman was respected as one of the best platoon and squad leaders. He was a wonderful guy. It was obvious that it hurt him to lose a man under his command.

Bobby George was a good guy from Tennessee. However, he was new and I did not get to spend much time with him.

Don Stewart was an old-timer from Harland County, Kentucky. I latched on to Don early on at LZ "Sally" before they dropped us off at firebase "Whip" at the south end of the A Shau Valley. That's the first thing they told us, "Grab you an old-timer and follow his lead." I became Don Stewart's shadow, following in his footsteps wherever he led—especially in battle. He was a real soldier and a close friend.

There was a clean-cut soldier by the name of Arlen Sieg who carried the M-60 machine gun for our squad. He did not talk much, but he was a trustworthy fellow on whom we could all depend.

And I can't forget Craig Simeone from Cohasset, Massachusetts, who was only with us for a month or two. He was a smart young man who was engaged to be married when he returned from his tour of duty. Craig was quiet but friendly. I remember that he would share his care packages that he received from his mother, June.

It made me sad to see new replacements come to the booneys because I knew what awaited them. I had no desire

to become attached to any of the new guys. It was too difficult to say "goodbye" when the time came and the time
always came one way or another. Of course, I was happy
to see guys I knew get to go home, but it tore a piece of my
heart out when they left.

Fear Takes Its Toll

As bad as actual combat really was, I don't think that's
what affected me the most. I know that it was living in
constant fear that tore away at me each day I lived in it. The
sounds of death, the smell of death, the feeling of death;
all these continued to tear at me over the years. I have kept
many of these things to myself, but every now and then I
remember it all so clearly.

Just the other day, I was walking to my truck at work.
The wooded area close by was really thick and green. I make
this walk every day and I have flashbacks of the jungles of
Vietnam. The smell carries me back in time and I can almost
hear the sounds of AK-47's popping in the distance. I look
through the thick and dark green foliage and so many memories of Vietnam come to mind. I can almost taste the sweat
and pick up on the distinct odor of the green army towel
around my neck. Often I have just wanted to sit down and
cry. However, when I think about what I had witnessed as
real heroes gave their lives for our country, I cannot allow
myself to just break down. Instead, I just think about how
grateful I am to still have an opportunity to make a difference in this life.

It hurt back then knowing nobody would ever know what
we experienced. Even when I returned to America, I felt as
if I wasn't worthy to talk about my time in Vietnam. My
thoughts were, *I lived through it when other men died so do
I really have the right?* I know our government has tried to
make it up to us in the past few years. But what I really want

to make clear now is how the Lord is giving back to me. I want this world to know that there is a Healer! He is a healer of wounds. He is a healer of hearts. He is a healer of minds and emotions. He is the God who heals.

CHAPTER 3

Combat
Has Its Price

———

Going into combat was always tough on a man's mind. In a combat assault situation, our company would be dropped into what we called a "hot LZ," which was a landing zone under heavy fire from the enemy. This was a rough situation—gut-wrenching. It was enough to make a man want to go AWOL. Of course, no one wanted to go into combat, but we were spurred on by the sacrifices we had already seen. It was different for the new guys. There was only fear.

Our company was often ordered to move into a firebase that had been previously overrun by the NVA—sometimes just the night before. I clearly remember when we were choppered in to a firebase "Airborne" which had been overrun the night before. In an attempt to offer support the night before, we had been moving toward the firebase through the undergrowth and darkness, but had not reached it in time to offer any help. There were no roads where we were, and we had to wait until the next morning to be air-lifted into the area by helicopter. We could hear the sounds of fighting coming from the distant firebase and knew that things were getting rough for our guys, but there was little that we could do to get there any faster in the darkness of the jungle.

I never will forget when they dropped us off that next morning. As I came off the chopper, what I saw would be forever burned into my mind. Seeing the emotional and physical condition of the men who had fought all night, not knowing if they would live to see the morning, just did something to us as soldiers. There was a connection between us and them. They had experienced the same fear we had, the same horror that we dreaded, and it was written all over their faces. We both had walked through the same valley and had known the same dark night. We were brothers even if we did not know their names.

As some of us entered a bunker in the compound in which we were to stay while there, the reality of what the men had faced was everywhere. The bunker still bore the splattered blood stains of the men who had occupied it and died in it the night before. It was our job to occupy the firebase until it could be reoccupied later by other forces. Then we would move on. But for now, we were to live among the many signs of death and destruction that surrounded us.

I remember so much about what I saw in the character of these men while in battle—things that you and I would not ordinarily see. It was remarkable. It was like everyone cared for one another. You were fighting for one another. Men were giving their lives for one another. Surviving was everything.

As we surveyed the destruction in the compound, we could not help but think of the wives, the children, and the families of these men who had held their ground valiantly and fought side-by-side with one another to the end. They fought for survival. They fought for one another and many of them died for one another. They fought and died because their country asked that of them. Still, it was for one another and to see another day with their families that they fought the hardest.

Although the exceptional valor of many of the men on the line was never reported, and though they did not get the awards they deserved, to be surrounded by them in combat was to know the meaning of true heroes.

Growing Up In the Booneys

It was March 1969, and we were in the A Shau Valley. We were involved in "Operation Massachusetts Striker." My squad, led by Sergeant Testerman, was the point squad that day, which meant that we were ahead and leading the rest of our company.

Robert Watt was walking as point man for the squad. Just as we started up the ridge, we were ambushed. The NVA had the high ground and AK-47's and machine gun fire as well as Rocket Propelled Grenades (RPGs) and satchel charges. The firefight was fierce. The deafening sound of the weapons, the confusion, and the fear of being killed were overwhelming.

Initially, I had taken cover behind a fallen tree that lay across a bomb crater along side of another guy named Arlen Sieg who was firing the M-60 machine gun. Don Stewart was on my other side. Suddenly, as I turned to look at Sieg I saw three rounds hit him in the head and then his head went down. Just that quickly I knew he was dead. I had been in firefights before but I had never seen casualties up close. It had always been someone that had not been near me. The sight of Sieg being hit right next to me really unnerved me, and fear took hold of me.

Just then, Don Stewart, an "old timer" who had been there three months longer than I yelled for me to "Leave him alone!" and to follow him. Watt had continued up the ridge firing his M-16, and others were following. I did as I was told and fell in behind Stewart, firing my M-16. Even so, I followed and had only gone a short distance when I was hit in the hip with shrapnel. When the shrapnel ripped into me

I was terrified to look to see the damage that it had done to my body.

Right away, I fell to the ground and yelled that I had been hit. I did not know what exactly had hit me, but I knew that I had been wounded.

A soldier in the company that I did not know stopped immediately, whirled around and knelt down to see how badly I had been wounded. I never will forget his face. He was a black soldier with lighter skin. He had a reddish tint to his hair and freckles were slightly visible on his face. He asked where I had been hit and I pointed to my hip. With one quick motion, he reached down and ripped my pants open where the fabric of my pants was torn. "Aw man, you just got a hole in you! You're alright!" he responded, much to my amazement.

I looked down to see the hole in my hip and steam rising from the hole in my body. I had been hit by shrapnel. As I lay there stunned, trying to grasp what had happened, I could not believe that the guy was so unconcerned. There was a hole in me! I wanted someone to have pity on me—to at least express some concern.

"Crawl back down the hill to the medic!" Stewart shouted. And with that he returned to the advance up the hill. Probably only seconds or only a couple of minutes had passed, but it seemed longer.

As I turned to crawl back down the ridge thinking about myself and remembering Sieg, I was still stunned. Within only a few minutes, all this had taken place. It was terrifying to see a man shot and killed right next to me, so close it could have been me. So unreal because we had just been talking minutes before the bullets ripped him away from me.

But really I was focused mainly on me—my pain and my fear. But there was no one there to comfort me or to pity me.

To my amazement, when I reached the bottom of the hill, there sat Sieg leaned up against a tree holding his steel pot in his hand, with three distinct holes where the rounds had struck the metal shell. There was a slight smile on his weary face as he said calmly, "I'm going home." His other wounds were sufficient to warrant a trip home, but the holes in his steel pot were the only evidence that he had been hit in the head. The rounds had evidently ricocheted upward as they hit the steel pot.

To my horror, there lay "Pop," I don't know his real name—never did—there wasn't time. We just called him "Pop"—because he was a few years older than we were—probably only in his mid-twenties. The blood coming from Pop's head and the darkness of the skin on his face told the unmistakable story that he had been hit in the head. His face had a black and blue color to it and it was evident that he was dead. Pop's limp body lay there on the ground cradled in the arms of a weeping Sergeant Bowman, who just sat there almost motionless holding Pop in his arms.

And there I was with a hole in my hip. I would live to see another day. They never even took the shrapnel out of me. It is in my abdomen to this day. At the hospital in Phu Bai, they just packed the hole with gauze until it healed.

Later the medivack chopper lifted Sieg and me out of the jungle. Then they lifted Pop out in a basket. Sieg and I went on to the hospital at Phu Bai, where I recovered from my wounds. Sieg was sent on to yet another hospital and I lost track of him.

That was the day I grew up. There was no one in the booneys to pet or pity me. Either way I gave up my need for it that day.

Temporary Diversions

While I was recovering from my wound at the hospital in Phu Bai, there was a great deal of time to kill and it could get pretty boring. To offset this, the hospital would schedule short boxing matches for those who were at the end of their recovery and who felt strong enough. It was exercise and entertainment. The prize for the winner was a case of Coca Cola and an opportunity to kiss one of the pretty nurses or one of the "Doughnut Dollies" there at the hospital. That was all the encouragement that I needed.

Some of the guys who were there recovering with me talked me into signing up to get in the ring. With their encouragement and the promise of a case of Cokes and a kiss from a pretty girl, I was primed by the time the match came around.

The fellow they paired me with was a tall, lean fellow that I thought I could take pretty easily. After all, it was only three rounds, and I was a fairly tough guy. We met in the ring, which amounted to a square formed from sand bags that had been stacked up about three feet high to form a boxing ring. The bell rang for the first round and I sailed into him like a tornado! I was hitting him everywhere and it appeared that he could barely respond to the onslaught. The first round ended with me more tired than I expected but clearly in control of the match.

However, when the bell rang for the second round, even with the encouragement from my friends, I could barely keep my arms up. My arms felt heavy and sluggish and, much to my concern, the other guy began to fight back. Maybe he wasn't as much of a pushover as I had thought. Maybe that was his strategy. Maybe he had just been letting me wear myself out. Either way, my arms were getting heavier by the minute and he was landing more punches so I just grabbed him and held on. I was literally hanging on around his waist in exhaustion. I wasn't landing any punches, but I was about to pull his shorts down if I got any more weary. When the referee would break us apart, I would grab on again. The second round ended and I was really worried.

By the time the bell rang for the beginning of the third round, I could not raise my hands above my waist. I was defenseless! How was I going to protect myself? On the other hand the other guy was ready to fight. I tried holding on to him, but he was hitting me in the back and the side of the head. The referee would break us apart and I would lunge for him in hopes of grabbing hold once again. Unfortunately for me, he got a clean shot at me before I could grab on and he hit me square on the chin. He hit me *hard* on the chin. I saw stars and black spots and went backward over the sand bags. All the while that bunch of guys who had gotten me into this mess was still egging me on. But it was over.

The round ended and they ruled the match a tie. I was happy that I would still get a half of a case of Cokes and still get to kiss a nurse! My happiness soon turned to disappointment when the nurse appeared. She must have weighed three hundred pounds if she weighed an ounce! I took the Cokes and went to get some rest.

CHAPTER 4

Hamburger Hill

———

It was between 12:30 and 1:00 a.m. in the early morning hours of the latter part of May 1969, the last day of the infamous eleven day battle. We were lying in the thick mud at our post wrapped in our poncho liners. We were on a lower ridge of the hill later to be named for its bloody aftermath— Hamburger Hill. Our ponchos partly shielded us from the blowing rain. Still the mud was inescapable. A heavy mist would settle on the mountains and ridge tops when it would rain, making it even more difficult to see.

We had been there several days. Our platoon had previously been at a base camp across the valley on a hill called "Eagle's Nest" when on May 10th Alpha Company of the 3/187th had initially discovered what was essentially an R and R station or outpost dug into the mountain. It was just off the Ho Chi Minh Trail and a perfect location for NVA troops moving down from up north to stop and rest and get re-supplied. A maze of underground tunnels dug into the mountain had previously concealed their presence and now made it very difficult to root them out of their hiding place. They had the high ground, they had underground bunkers, they had supplies, and they had a tenacious determination to hold their position.

Every day our platoon had watched from the other side of the valley as the sky above the valley and mountains were filled with jets dropping bombs during the day trying to clear out the NVA forces from their placements. Our platoon was securing Eagles Nest. The rest of our company, Bravo Company 2/501st, was already there. After being spectators for several days and hoping that we would not be needed, we received the call to enter the battle and help take the hill. The hill was actually more of a mountain top. It was the Ap Bia Mountain in the A Shau Valley. There were soldiers from Alpha Company 3/187th, 2/506th, Bravo Company 1/506th, 2/501st, Charlie Company 3/187th, 1/506th, two companies from the South Vietnamese Army, 3/ARVN and others fighting their way up the hill from all sides. We were on the northeast ridge.

On this particular night it was my squad's turn to be on ambush duty. We had taken up our position about seventy-five yards uphill from the remainder of our company. Our job was to watch for NVA troops that might be making their way down the hill under cover of night with the intent of ambushing our company.

The weather was terrible: rain, fog, no visibility. It was the most dangerous of conditions. We lay there waiting for the unknown to make itself known. It was an unbelievably tense situation because we knew things could get really bad, really quickly if the NVA made a move. No sooner had our minds gone through the possible scenarios than the trip-flares around our perimeter began going off to the right of our position.

Our first thought was that possibly the rainy weather could have tripped the flairs. We were wrong. It was the NVA. Unknown to us, Sergeant Testerman had sent Watt to move around the perimeter to our right. This is what initiated the contact with the NVA who were moving in on our position. Without any further warning they opened up on us and began throwing satchel charges in our direction. Sergeant

Testerman, who was nearby, yelled to us, "Don't blow the claymores!" His concern was that the NVA may have gotten within our lines and turned our claymores in on us. If this were the case and we blew them, we would be killed by our own mines. (Claymore mines are above ground mines that explode in the outward direction in which they are pointed.)

I remember that the man next to me was Douglas Wineglass. Wineglass had an M-16 and I had Sieg's old M-60 machine gun that he had left behind after he had been wounded. Wineglass and I were firing as rapidly as we could in the direction of what we thought to be the location of the NVA. My M-60 kept misfiring and jamming. At one point I was blown away from it by the blast of a satchel charge, but I was able to find it again. In all the movement, the M-60 machine gun that I had been firing became so caked with mud that it eventually stopped firing. It was now useless. The rain and lack of visibility was disorienting. The darkness was interrupted from time to time with the glare from the flares and the continuous explosions that eventually made it impossible to know everything that was happening or even where everyone was.

We could hear Sergeant Testerman screaming for help over the radio as he called just down the hill to the rest of our company. He probably could have been heard by them without the radio. Wineglass had run out of ammo at this point; he and I were now both without a weapon in our possession that would fire. We tossed every grenade we had — at that point we only had God to call on. Hearing Robert Watt yelling for help from a position just a few yards down the hill, we tried to make our way to him. We knew that he had been wounded and was evidently unable to move, but we still could not see him. We could only hear him calling from the darkness and confusion, and there appeared to be no way to get to him no matter how hard we tried. Any movement toward Watt was met with heavy fire from the NVA.

Sergeant Testerman called out from the surrounding darkness and told Bobby George and me to try to crawl down the hill and get to Watt if we could. I had no weapon so I began to crawl down the hill behind Bobby. I was crawling so close behind Bobby that I was almost between his feet when I heard a round hit him and I heard him cry out. The incoming fire was too intense. We had to pull back or we would have been killed. Perhaps we could reach him later.

The remainder of our company could not get to us and we could not get to them. We were in "no man's land"—cut off and being overrun. Because it was night and the weather was so bad, there would be no air support to save us. We were on our own and were not sure if we would end up as POWs or dead.

The CO, Captain Kurt Franzinger, took a chance and told Sergeant Testerman to get off the hill. In fact, the order he shouted was, "Get off the hill any way you can!" Clearly, it was up to us to get off the hill by any means possible. In fact, if it had not been for the order given by the CO for us to get off the hill any way we could, we would have certainly all been killed. Although we knew four or five men were still on the hill dead or severely wounded, we were helpless to do anything about it. Eventually, a few of us made it off the hill in the darkness and chaos, though I do not know how. Some were left behind, like Robert Watt. We could not help him. Nothing would work. The lines were so crossed and confused that if we fired wildly in the darkness and confusion at what we thought was the NVA, we might hit our own men.

The haunting memory of Watt calling out to us for help will always be with me. It was maddening that every time someone would start out on his own to attempt to reach Watt, he would get hit and Watt would remain beyond our reach. Thinking back on the situation, I believe that, unknown to Watt, the NVA had surrounded him and when he would call out and someone would start for him they were sitting ready to pick us off one at a time.

We continued to fight all night long. We could hear "Puff," an airplane with mini-machine guns, circling above us, but there was no way he could know our position and that of the NVA because of the cloud cover. At one point on my way down the hill, I jumped into a foxhole knee deep in water with the CO and his radio operator (RTO). The RTO shouted to me that there was not enough room for me; however, I had no weapon and nowhere else to hide so I was coming in that foxhole with them!

I was in the foxhole long enough to hear them trying to contact our squad's RTO, Armendariz. When morning came and the process of recovering the dead and wounded had started, we found that Armendariz had been badly wounded and had almost bled to death on the hill that night. During the night, unsure of his fate, the CO took a chance and called over the radio to Armendariz in hopes of finding out if he was still alive. Calling over the radio he asked, "If you score a basket in basketball, how many points do you get?" Someone on the other end holding the squelch button on the radio popped the squelch twice. We were pretty sure it had to be him and that he was alive. Later he told us that he had lain there all night pretending to be dead as the NVA soldiers crawled over his body as they moved across the hill.

While trying to make it off the hill, the explosions continued to throw us about as we were bombarded by mortar fire and anything else that they could throw at us. Once down the hill, I remember sitting at the base of a large tree between the big roots that protruded above the ground and holding on to them like a man would hold to the arms of a chair while virtually being blown from my only place of refuge. With each explosion my grip would tighten on the roots as I tried to endure one more blast in the continuing barrage that I thought would never end. We prayed for the light of the morning because we could see nothing. There was little that we could do but hold on and pray for morning light, when air support and the support of other companies could be called in on our position. For those of us who had been on the hill with our squad, we had to spend the remainder of the night wrestling with the fact that some of our squad members were still on the hill, unknown to us whether they were dead or alive. Either way, we could do nothing.

When the dawn finally arrived, we were all the same in the morning light. We all looked the same—covered in mud, blood and with that far off stare. We did not know who all was missing from our company. But many of the men I had lived with and laughed with, read mail with, lay dead on "Hamburger Hill." These are images that are forever etched in my mind. In fact, I can still see them clearly today.

Much to my amazement I came off Hamburger Hill alive but with shrapnel in my legs and in my arms. Perhaps the biggest injury I suffered that night was shock. Looking back, maybe I was having a breakdown. I do not know. All I know is that I could not stop shaking. The convulsive shaking of my body was so bad that one guy actually tried lying on top of me to hold me down and to get my body to stop shaking.

When the night was over I found that Captain Kurt Franzinger, a West Point graduate and a man I greatly admired, also survived that night. But sadly, he was killed two or three weeks later by a rocket propelled grenade (RPG) that hit him squarely in the chest. Bobby George had also survived, as did Sergeant Dave Testerman. Arlen Sieg had already gone home and Don Stewart was on R and R during that time or else he would have been right there in the middle of it. Tragically, another good friend, Craig Simeone, was shot in the forehead while we were being overrun on Hamburger Hill. He died there beside Robert Watt, as did Sergeant Edwin Dotter from Wichita, Kansas, and Louis Johnson from St. Louis.

CHAPTER 5

Little Joe

After Hamburger Hill my squad was gone. It had been dismantled by attrition. The guys I was so close to were now dead, transferred or sent home. The thought of going into battle without the men who had become like brothers to me was more than I could face. Fortunately, Ronnie McCrary, a friend from my home town, talked to Captain Bradshaw about getting me into the 47th Infantry Scout Dog Platoon of the 101st Airborne Division. It would mean that I would have to extend my tour of duty an extra six months, but I thought that it would be worth it. It would be better than going back into battle, having had to start all over again with new guys. At least this way, being paired with a scout dog, I would not have to get close to another human being. Little did I know that the dog they paired me with, Little Joe, would become just as much a friend as those guys I had served with previously. So, I made my decision to transfer to the scout dog platoon and Ronnie extended with me. Now that is a real friend.

Ronnie and Wade

I did get to go home for a short visit back in the States, and almost did not make it back for my new assignment. While on leave I got in a fight with some guys. I was in the wrong place at the wrong time and when it was all over, they had beaten me up pretty bad and broken my arm. But I could not let Ronnie go back without me, because his sole reason for extending his tour was to serve with me. There was nothing left to do but to make the best of it. When time came for me to go back, I just cut the cast off my arm and went on. I knew if the Army found out that my arm was broken, they would delay my return and reassign me. It took some doing and enduring some pain when I got back to Vietnam, but I covered up the fact that the arm was broken until it had healed.

A New Friend

Little Joe

Little Joe was a German shepherd, just about three years old. He had already been trained back in the States before ever coming to Vietnam. He was to become my new best friend and fellow soldier. As I would learn, the relationship between a dog handler and his dog is unique and special. The dog is not the soldier's pet. The dog is viewed as his fellow soldier and friend.

From the beginning Little Joe and I were inseparable. It was important to build a strong relationship between the handler and the dog. That relationship was everything. The life of both could depend upon it. As a result, I did all that I could to strengthen our bond. We slept side by side, ate side by side, trained side by side and went into battle as one.

Me and Little Joe

Although I had never gone through the dog handler's school at Fort Benning, Georgia, Little Joe had been well trained, which made it easier for me to learn to work with him. Scout dogs are disciplined animals. They are not the aggressive attack dogs that some people may think of when they envision a German shepherd in military service. It was our job to walk point in certain situations so that Little Joe would have the opportunity to sniff out the enemy. When he detected something he would alert on the possible position of the enemy. His alert was clear to me. He would stop in his tracks and begin to lift his head slowly. His ears would perk up and he would begin to cock his head to the side a bit and sniff the air. Other than that, he would hardly move. I would quickly get down as soon as he alerted and begin to whisper to him. By watching his slightest movements, I could read him as if I knew what he was trying to say to me.

Periodically he would turn his head and make eye contact with me—not for instructions—he was looking out for me. He was always taking care of me and making sure that I knew that there was danger. If he ever sensed imminent danger, he would hesitate about coming all the way back to me. He wanted to stay between me and whatever might harm me.

One instance in which the value of a scout dog was demonstrated was the day we got a call to send in a scout dog to find a Long Range Reconnaissance Patrol (LRRP) squad. Little Joe and I had just returned from four or five days in the field and were looking forward to a time of rest. After that many days in the field, all I wanted was to have a shower and get some sleep. I had just lain down on my bunk when a soldier came in and said that my CO, Lieutenant (later Captain) James Bradshaw, wanted Little Joe and me on the double. He said for me to get Little Joe, an M-16, and some ammo and meet him at the helicopter pad.

The LRRP's were doing reconnaissance when they were spotted by the enemy. The NVA was closing in on their position, but were still searching for their exact location. We had to find the team before the NVA did, and Lt. Bradshaw knew that Little Joe could find them first. We had the general coordinates of their location. Troup positions were plotted on a grid, but the recon squad had to remain under cover until we arrived to assist them in getting out. Without us they had no support. The difficult thing for the team was that they had to stay under cover without making their exact position known to anyone until we made contact with them.

We loaded into one of the two choppers along with several other soldiers and took off. Once we landed, Joe and I walked point. The helicopters took off again and remained airborne for safety while keeping a lock on our position. Walking point in the jungle was something else—stressful and unnerving. In the mountain areas, walking point was a dangerous proposition. Words cannot adequately describe the feeling. Anytime contact was made with the enemy, it was that initial burst of machine gunfire that would often get the point man or members of the point squad.

It felt a little better if you had a scout dog with you. The dog would be out in front of everyone and could pick up on any suspicious movement or presence more quickly than a man. Unlike with some dogs I could work Little Joe off a leash. He was a disciplined animal. He would walk as far as he could in front of me without losing clear sight of me. He would not go too far ahead. If he felt he was too far ahead, he would stop and wait for me to get closer. As long as I could see him, I could read his movements and tell what he was thinking.

Once on the ground in search of the LRRP squad, it took Little Joe only twenty to thirty minutes until he had found them. Finding them so quickly saved their lives and ours too.

Little Joe and I were inseparable for six months, but tragedy soon struck. It was an extremely hot and humid day, late one afternoon, almost nightfall. We were on a trail in the A Shau Valley not too far from Firebase Blaze.

That morning Little Joe and I had been walking point for a small squad that was out on a reconnaissance patrol for the 3rd Platoon Delta Company, 1st Battalion of the 501st Infantry.

Joe had alerted strongly on some NVA soldiers twice that morning. We even found evidence of where the NVA had come down the hill. There was broken brush and other signs where they had slid down the hill. But, since that particular Commanding Officer was new in the field, he saw no need to call in the Cobra gunships. He did not think Little Joe had actually detected anything so his only precaution was to tell us to "shoot up the hill." Since we did not draw any enemy fire by doing this, he mistakenly thought it was safe to resume the patrol in that area. He then took me and Little Joe off point until that afternoon.

Later that afternoon he called me to the front to walk point again as the whole company was going up the next ridge. Half-way up the hill Little Joe alerted strong and once more and I pulled him back to go report to the CO that Little Joe had detected the enemy nearby. Nevertheless, the CO wanted to send Little Joe and me back up again ahead of the column. The CO told me that he wanted me to go a little further this time. I told him again in no uncertain terms and less respectfully than the first time, that the enemy was there. Little Joe did not lie. Nevertheless, he said, "I'm giving you a direct order to get back on the point and get up that ridge!" All my warnings had fallen on deaf ears.

A little farther up the hill, Joe was maybe twenty feet in front of me as we started back up the ridge. Suddenly, he alerted. At the instant he alerted, the NVA opened up on us from a bunker up the ridge! We had been going uphill and the NVA had taken a position uphill from us and had the advantage of firing downhill at us. As I dove for the ground, I hit the quick release on my rook sack so that I could get free of it. The guy walking my "slack," not too far behind me moved forward and dove down almost beside me. He had not freed himself from his rook sack, and the incoming rounds were so close that the c-ration cans in his rook sack were being hit.

At first I saw a few of the muzzle blasts, and then I could see nothing for keeping my head down.

The angle of fire from the NVA's bunker made it possible for us to stay under their fire. To get a better angle on us, they would have had to leave their bunker position in order to shoot straight down on us. This would have left them exposed and thankfully they were not willing to take that chance. They remained in their position and thus the fire continued to pass just above our heads for the most part.

We were pinned down flat on our stomachs and could not even rise up or else we would be hit. We remained pinned down for about fifteen minutes before we could do anything. It seemed like hours. At times I think that I lost all sensation of feeling anything, the fear was so intense. The guys farther down the hill from us saved us because from their position they could return fire. All that I could think of was that Little Joe was missing.

I knew something was wrong because Little Joe would usually hunker down and crawl back to me once the shooting started. I was pretty sure that he may have been hit, but I could not see him, and he had not returned. It was almost dark by the time the NVA disengaged us and we were able to make it up the hill to where they had been. As we reached the top of the hill where the NVA had been firing down on us, we found Little Joe's body riddled with bullets. Apparently, while we were pinned down—unable to move or see all that was happening—Little Joe had attacked their position. Somehow he managed to reach their position and had done what he could do to aid and defend his fellow soldiers. Now he lay covered in blood with his wounds clearly visible.

What made matters worse was that I could not reach out and take him in my arms as I wanted to do. We knew that the NVA may have booby trapped his body by rigging explosives to his body, set to explode when we moved him. It was a common tactic of the enemy and one more indignity for a valiant soldier. Carefully we tied a rope to his legs, then after withdrawing a safe distance, we gently pulled his body from where it lay. Thankfully there were no explosives. Now it was time to take my fallen friend from the battlefield. I loaded Little Joe into a "Huey" helicopter and we flew on to Firebase Blaze. From there, the two of us took a Chinook helicopter and flew on to LZ Sally where I buried him.

Initially the CO did not even want me to take Little Joe's body back with us. He wanted to just leave him in the field—discarded like a useless weapon. However, men from the company volunteered to carry him back to the LZ. They cut down a small sapling and, tying his feet together, they slipped the sapling between his legs, lifted him up, and carried him back down the trail to where he could be loaded on the helicopter.

Little Joe should have been awarded a medal that day because his actions saved at least ten men's lives. But the CO would have had to admit that he was wrong about Joe and that he had ignored repeated warnings.

I have thought a good bit about the way Little Joe died, and I think, in a way, that I am glad that he died the way that he did. The Army did not bring the scout dogs home and retire them. Had he not died in combat, when the Army was finished with him, they would have just discarded him by putting him to sleep. He deserved to die a hero's death.

CHAPTER 6

Back
in the USA

I really do not know what I thought of America when I got back home from my tour in Vietnam. It was difficult for me to feel that I fit in any more. My world was different and America seemed so different from the time when I had first left. The anti-war comments from the Vietnam War protestors were different now that I had been there and been a part of fighting America's "unpopular" war.

Their comments stung me and angered me mainly because when they trashed the soldiers of Vietnam, spat on us, or treated us with contempt—they were not just doing it to me—they were doing that to my friends who fought and died in Vietnam. They were not just insulting me, they were insulting good men who had died for their country and served their country with loyalty and honor—even though it was not "popular" to do so.

I hate war. Those who have actually fought wars always do. There is nothing that a protestor, politician, or an activist can do to cause me to dislike war any more than I do. In fact, if they have never been there in the blood and terror fighting for survival, they have nothing to say to me. I do not glory in war. I just refuse to allow the memory and honor of good men to be spoken of despairingly by those who did not even understand or care about what we had endured.

It just bothered me that no one would know, or wanted to know for that matter, what we had been through and what the war had done to us. It was the idea that no one would appreciate the sacrifices of my friends who died in Vietnam and the trauma that I and many others had endured that fueled my resentment and anger when I returned home.

Consequently, the turmoil I felt after being back in the States kept me on edge and more sensitive to the feeling that all my friends and I had gone through was viewed by some as meaningless. I rebelled in small ways at first. For instance, when I returned home I was supposed to report to the Veteran's Hospital in Birmingham because of my previous wounds and the fact that I still had shrapnel in me. But I refused. I wanted nothing to do with the government.

Rebellion Sets In

Consequently, I had little respect for civil authority. On one such occasion in our small town that lack of respect led me to some risky behavior. The police pulled me over while I was driving my father's car and told me that I had unpaid fines in my name. They would have to arrest me.

In response, I told them that I was not going to jail. They said I was. I said I wasn't. It did not take long before they had thrown me into the backseat of the patrol car and were headed for the county jail with me in spite of my protest. Up till then things had not been going my way, but that changed when they chose not to put me in handcuffs. Evidently they did not consider me to be a threat.

As they drove I searched my mind trying to devise a plan. Surveying the situation, I saw that the patrol car was new and they had not yet removed the inside door handles from the rear doors as was the normal procedure. Before they could get to the four-lane highway where the speed limit was higher, I would jump out of the patrol car. We did not seem to be going too fast, and I thought that I would just hit and roll as I came out of the car. We had not gone too far down the road when I made my move. I grabbed the door handle and pushed my way out of the car to freedom. I hit and I rolled and I flipped end over end. I thought I would never stop flipping.

When I did stop I was lying in a ditch flat of my back. Much to my amazement, I was not hurt—just scratched a little. Unfortunately, there had been a state trooper traveling along not far behind the patrol car, and when he saw me come out of the car, he pulled over and stopped immediately. It would do me no good to run now, so I just lay there like I was hurt.

Soon the officers that had arrested me and the trooper were standing over me. As one reached out to take hold of me, the trooper yelled, "Don't touch him! You were doing at least fifty miles an hour when he jumped out. He could be hurt bad." My backup plan was working so I just lay there.

Not wanting to take any more chances with this nut, and since they had been responsible for me while I was in their custody, they called for an ambulance. I continued to lay there motionless. As I had said, I wasn't going to jail. They could just take me to the hospital and I would escape from there.

As it turned out, the ambulance driver was a guy I knew. His nickname was "Goat." Once in the back of the ambulance with the doors shut, Goat was startled when I came to life, opened my eyes, and asked "Hey, Goat, you got a cigarette?" Surprised he responded, "Wade, you're a nut!"

Possibly they were afraid of being sued, but they never picked me up from the hospital to take me to jail. They did send my father the hospital bill, but he just sent it back to them telling them that they had been responsible for not securing me properly in the patrol car. We never heard anything else about it and I didn't go to jail. I told them I wasn't going to jail.

Finding the Right Path Was Difficult

People's actions could set me off easily. In those days I often hung out with my good friend, Ronnie. Like me, Ronnie was a young man with little patience for being mistreated. Like me, he was quick to respond to any aggravation, and he was eager to handle almost any that came his way. He was not scared of anything or anybody. The bigger they were the bigger the challenge.

Once, when we were shooting pool in a bar in Huntsville, the guy I was playing mouthed off to me so I took the pool cue and hit him across the face. It stunned him pretty good, and he stumbled backward and began covering for the next blow that he assumed was coming. I was just about ready to continue my work with the pool cue when, unknown to me, the bar bouncer approached me from behind. Before I could take another swing, the bouncer took a lead-filled stick called a "slap-jack," and he hit me in the back of the head hard enough to knock the taste out of my mouth!

Immediately, I hit the floor of that bar stunned. As I turned to see where Ronnie was, I saw that he had taken up the fight where I had left off and was using the pool balls as weapons. Throwing them like baseballs, he was pelting the guy I had hit and threatening to do the same to anyone who approached him. No one would go near him—until that is—he ran out of pool balls. The police were on the way so I started crawling for the door. I had had enough and I had no plans of going to jail. I headed to the hotel room I had across the street, but Ronnie still wanted to fight, and the police ended up getting him and hauling him to jail.

Until then bar fights, drinking and doing some drugs had been the worst of my adventures. But there was that underlying feeling of frustration with people, perhaps in general, that continued to draw my life off course, and one night, it almost went horribly wrong.

It was a day like most, but on this day some guys we knew had stolen a bunch of our stuff out of our car and we were going to get even. Four other guys and I were a little high and the wrong that had been done to us had inspired us to get even. That evening, after dark, we drove to where these guys lived who had done us wrong. The people we were after were having a party. The house was full. The plan was for some of the other guys to flush them out of the house, and Billy and I were simply going to shoot the guilty members of the party.

Parked outside their house I sat in the front seat of the car and loaded my 30/06 rifle. One of the other guys with me, Billy, had a 30/30 rifle. As we prepared to get our revenge, he decided that he would crawl into the back seat so that he could get a better shot out of the back window. He crawled over the seat into the back seat and began trying to get a round in the chamber. The rifle was jamming, and he struggled to get a round in the chamber. Just as he succeeded, the rifle accidentally went off, sending a bullet toward me in the front seat. I felt something hit my leg and knew that he had inadvertently shot me. I felt my leg and could tell that I was bleeding. Our presence then was known and people came running out of their houses. We took off out of there and headed for the hospital. As it turned out, the bullet had ripped into the console of the car and it was a fragment of the console and not the bullet that had gone into my leg.

In reality, it was the best thing that could have happened. In the state of mind that I was in and with the drugs that were in my system, I would have surely killed someone that night if that little accident had not happened. If the rifle had been pointed a little more to the left, then I would have been killed myself. It was the grace of God that kept me from completely ruining the rest of my life and someone else's too.

The ironic thing is that I never intended for my life to get as messed up as it was. Even from a child, I always wanted to be a good person. On that night, had it not been for what I believe to be God's intervention, I would have most likely spent the last thirty years in prison. Instead, I would go on to see God do some great things in my life in spite of momentary unwillingness to listen to His voice calling me to Him.

CHAPTER 7

Fighting a Losing Battle

———

In spite of my feelings about people in general, I was not always angry. Some days were good. Most days I had no plans for doing anything wrong, but it seemed that trouble was pursuing me. For instance, one day some friends of mine had taken me fishing. We were out on the lake in their boat enjoying the peaceful day catching fish and having a good time. After we had fished a while, the game warden came by checking fishing licenses. Well, I had not even renewed my driver's license, much less gotten a fishing license when I returned home. Honestly, I just did not want anything to do with the government in any form any longer and I had decided that I was not going to sign up for anything—not even VA benefits at the veteran's hospital. Consequently, when the game warden asked for my fishing license, I had to tell him that I had none.

The guys with me tried to get him to let me off with a warning, telling him that I had just returned from Vietnam. "Well," the game warden responded, "I'll tell you what he should have done when he got back from Vietnam—he should have got him a fishing license." With that he proceeded to give me a ticket. This only made me angrier. His attitude just seemed to bring back old memories better off forgotten. He was a state official and obviously he thought very little of me and what I had done for our country. This only seemed to confirm my cynical feelings about the way things were. But then again, I had no intention of paying it, so I said nothing.

You might think that a game warden would have more to do than track down people who had not paid a fishing fine, but you would be wrong. A year-and-a-half later, I was swimming at a friend's apartment complex swimming pool when I saw that same game warden coming toward us. Sure enough, he arrested me for not paying the fine and threw me into jail.

After that episode I just went bad. I just did not seem to care anymore. I wanted out of my small town, so I started traveling. I would spend the next three or four years either drunk or high. First I went to Chicago, spending a month or so there, then on to St. Louis, Denver, Atlanta, Tampa and many other places along the way. I would work some and live where I could. I would stay at the Salvation Army or a flop house here and there. I have even slept under bridges when nothing else was available. If I had money, I was usually in a bar somewhere, drinking and playing pool.

Once on the road I was living free without a plan or a concern for the future. My good friend Noony was my traveling companion for many trips. We were both from the Huntsville area in North Alabama. From one rock festival to another we would travel—working here and there, staying where we could. I would go where I could, not necessarily like a homeless person we see today, but more like a drifter. Back then it was not unusual for someone to hike all over the country, bathing in rivers and streams, traveling wherever they chose to go.

Once, before returning to stay in Alabama, Noony and I set off hitchhiking from Atlanta all the way to the Rocky Mountains. Our destination was Grand Junction, Colorado.

One day not long after I reached the Rockies, it had gotten late and I had camped on a ridge close to the road near Denver, Colorado. That next morning I decided that I would bathe in a nearby stream as I had done many times before in other parts of the country. Little did I know that the water in the stream that ran down from the mountains above was produced largely from the melting ice and snow. I almost froze.

I did not like this way of life, but I just could not see my way out of where I had found myself. I know that my mother and my grandmother were praying for me all along the way.

When I was wandering around the country for those years, I never got drunk or high to forget. I always got high to remember. I did not want to forget. I know it took everybody serving in Vietnam no matter where they served or what branch in which they served. Yet, for those who constantly confronted the death and carnage, a close bond would form. The "ground-pounders" were the men with whom I identified and could never forget. So I drank or got high to remember.

It was not a good way to deal with the past, but it was my way of dealing with the past. I would just sit and drink and think about it—every detail, every battle—trying not to forget the men who never made it back, as well as all the men with whom I served.

When I came back to Huntsville, I was a wasted man. But the woman with whom I would be reunited and that I would later marry would be so good to me in spite of what I was at the time. I had not seen her in five years. Her name was Gail. I had always loved Gail as far back as high school. We had even dated some, but she was a good girl, beautiful, and from a well-to-do family. It seemed impossible that someone like her could ever really love someone like me. I knew that she thought I was good-hearted but just a bit of a "wild child." That is why when we did date in high school, we had to sneak around. As far as loving a girl, Gail was it.

CHAPTER 8

Life
Begins Again

———

I had not been back in Huntsville long when some of her friends told me that they had seen Gail and that she had asked about me and said that she would like to see me. She had written her phone number and address on a napkin and told them to give it to me if they saw me. It was soon there-after when I called her and told her that I would like to come see her. It was August of 1974. I remember that I showed up on her doorstep barefoot, wearing a cut-off t-shirt, long hair and pair of sunglasses. What I had on was all I had in the world, and I had been high on drugs and alcohol for the last four years. Although both of us had come from good families, in my present condition, I was not exactly what her family had hoped she would find. I was in rough shape, my life was in shambles, and I was on my last mile.

Gail's roommate answered the door. There's no telling what she thought. Gail was glad to see me, and after we talked awhile, she decided that she would cut my hair for me and carry me to the mall to buy me a pair of shoes and some clothes. That made me a little more presentable but did little to change her parents' minds about me. It was clear that I would never be the son-in-law of their dreams. Of course, I couldn't blame them; I was a mess. Years later all would be well, and I would be well thought of by them. Gail's father was a quiet man of few words and a good man, but not a man that it would be wise to cross. He worked for NASA and was always reading and kept to himself. Gail's mother was a good woman as well. She loved attention, but was also reserved. Their opinion of me changed so much that in 1994 I would have the opportunity to lead her dad to the Lord. He was eighty-one years old. Before her mother died, she asked me to deliver her eulogy at her funeral. A few months later, I would do the same for Gail's father. But early on it was just difficult for them to see past who I was at that first impression. It took Gail some time, but eventually she had improved my appearance and had me moving in the right direction.

It would not be but a few months before we would be on our way to getting married. Everyone thought that she had lost her mind. There was no house, no money, and no steady job for me. All the same, we were going to be married whether we had anything to our name or not. A fancy ceremony was out of the question so we planned to go to Trenton, Georgia.

It was October 1974. The morning we planned to get married we stopped by my parent's house, and I told my dad that Gail and I had planned on going to get married. He was surprised and a little doubtful of what I was telling him, so he asked Gail, "Is he telling the truth?" She assured him that I was, and he asked if we had any money. We told him that we didn't. "Well, I'll get you the money." He went in his bedroom and came out with some money for us to get married. I think that he was grateful that I was beginning to settle down and that I had found such a good woman.

We arrived that day in Trenton, Georgia, at the courthouse to be married. Once in the judge's chambers, the judge asked us if we wanted the short ceremony or the long one. I quickly said, "The short one." Consequently, before we knew it we were married. "Get you one of those bags over there," the judge said as he pointed to the corner of the room where several large paper bags were. We had seen people carrying those bags out of the courthouse when we came in, but we did not know what was in them.

The paper bag stood about two-and-a-half feet tall and in it we found everything from washing powders to aspirin—all the things a newlywed couple would need who didn't have anything. That was us, newly married with nothing to our name. We were in love, and I was going to be a different man.

Nevertheless, I still had a great deal of changing to do. I still had considerable contempt for the government because I had seen how they treated Vietnam veterans. My contempt for the law and the government was so intense that I did not even want to get a driver's license. I had never renewed them after I got back from Vietnam, but Gail persisted that if I were going to get a job, I would need a driver's license.

It was tough to learn to do the right things again, but Gail patiently coached me. She has always said that there is never been a dull moment in her life with me. In reality, my life had stopped after Vietnam, that is; until I met Gail again.

As I said earlier, when Gail and I started out we really had nothing to speak of—especially me. Gail had attended beauty school and was working. We lived with my mother and father at first, but after two months into our marriage we were finally able to rent a small house that we could call our own. It was a good thing because just three months after we were married Gail was pregnant with our daughter, Carmen.

Carmen was born on September 9, 1975 in the year after we were married. Things were getting better little by little, and once we had Carmen it seemed like everything was complete in our little family. God had given me the wife and the child that I thought I would never have when I was sitting in the jungles of Vietnam trying to imagine the future. At this point I think some people were amazed that we were actually making it. Many had not held out much hope for me to amount to anything. But God had not given up on me, and the family that He gave me was an added incentive to work and become a better man.

I wanted my daughter Carmen to know me as a good man and not the man that I had been in previous years. Carmen was a good-natured and beautiful child. Like any proud father I enjoyed showing her off any time we went somewhere. Over the years she has grown up to be a beautiful young woman, married to a good man, Charles Schrimsher. We just call him Buddy. And the added blessing is that we have three wonderful grandchildren: Taylor, Sam, and Autumn. When I look at them, I cannot help but to be reminded that the Lord has never forgotten me. It's not that I deserve what He has done for me; in fact, it is because that He has blessed me in spite of my unworthiness that makes the blessings even more wonderful!

Taylor, Carmen, Autumn, Buddy and Sam

We had not been married long until I was taking any job I could find. Drugs and alcohol had taken its toll on me physically, and it was hard to make the adjustment to a normal life of work and responsibility. Most of the work that I could get was hard labor, such as farm work. It was hard work for anyone and even harder for someone who had been drinking and doing drugs for the previous four years.

However, I kept working, trying to pull myself out of my condition. Occasionally, I would smoke some weed and drink some. I just assumed that drugs and alcohol would always be a part of my life. That was before I knew what was possible.

One day when Gail was watching the PTL television program, she responded to the invitation and accepted Jesus Christ as her Savior. As soon as I came in from work that day, I knew something was different. Something about Gail had changed. She was in the living room, and I came in and sat down with her, still resting my lunch box on my knee. As I sat there she began to tell me about Jesus and the love of God. She told me about praying and accepting Christ as her Savior, and then she told me that God loved me too and wanted me to give my life to him.

Although I did not feel that I was ready for church or God, I listened to what Gail had to say. It was only a day or two afterward I was on my way to work early in the morning. It was before daylight, and I was to meet up with the guy I rode to work with in Guntersville, Alabama. I began to pray. My prayer was simple. I said, "Dear Lord, I love Gail and I love Carmen, and I don't want to lose them. If somehow you will take me, that's what I am trying to ask you." I got back into my car and drove on to meet my ride. We went on to work, but I just could not get the Lord off my mind all day. Returning home my ride let me out, and once in my car, I started back home still feeling the need to pray. I remembered my parents taking me to church in my childhood. As a young child I remember lying under the pew eating crackers as my parents and the other people worshipped around me.

Once again I pulled over on the side of Highway 431, near Guntersville, Alabama. I remember that it was near Honeycomb Lake that I stopped and decided that I would try to pray. Leaving the door open, I knelt down and hid behind the door as I prayed. As I talked to God I told Him, "Lord, I remember as a child learning in Sunday School that You are the only one who can help me. If there is anyway that You will have me—then that is what I am trying to tell you." I then got back in my car and began to drive on toward home. Honestly, I felt a little silly once I was back in the car. What I had done seemed foolish, but I really meant it.

So, not being satisfied, I stopped again a couple of miles down the road, got out of my car and walked around to the other side and knelt down so that no one passing by would see me, and I began to pray again, "Lord, I have heard people talk about repenting. Lord, whatever that word repent means, I don't really know, but I want to say I'm sorry."

At that moment it seemed that heaven fell on me! I knew that God had heard my prayer and that things were going to be different. In fact, things were different. Although I never prayed about it, much to my delight and the surprise of others, I never drank, smoked weed, or took any more drugs from that day. When God saved me, He healed me completely.

Mistakenly, once I was in church again, I tried to take on the ultra strict lifestyle I had seen modeled by Christians I knew growing up in rural North Alabama. I had been raised in church by good parents. They were both loving people, yet my father took a hard line or legalistic approach to serving God. My mother was not so much that way, but my father set the tone in our house about how one should serve the Lord. It took me a couple of years, but soon I realized that I would have to find my way and see that living for God was about more than keeping rules.

Eventually I would begin to come out of that mindset in the years that followed. Marrying my wife Gail and accepting Jesus Christ into my life was a major turning point for me. Slowly, things began to happen that only God could bring about. For the first time I started enjoying being alive and enjoying doing normal things once again. Soon I began to think, *Maybe there is a way that I can do something with my life*. Things continued to change slowly. No longer did I sit and dwell on the past all the time. No more drinking, no drugs; I had a new life. Yet God had more in store for me that I would soon discover.

CHAPTER 9

God Moments

———

Once I had accepted Christ and had begun to live my new life, I had a great desire to share my faith and what had happened to me with those whom I had spent the previous years. I had always known that if I became a Christian, it would be all or nothing for me. However, since my previous years had been spent around drug addicts and people wanted by the law, it presented me with a challenge. Telling them about Jesus would be the easy part. But I did not want to be mistaken by the police as being a part of what was happening in those homes. In addition, it was dangerous to walk into those situations unannounced or unexpectedly if a man was not a part of that culture and aware of who was there and what was gong on at that time. It would be easy to get shot if I made the wrong move with the wrong person.

Knowing that was the case, I still was willing to take some risk to share this wonderful thing that had turned my life around, and I knew no one who needed it more than these people whom I had known. Many Saturday mornings I would set out in my car in search of someone to win to Jesus Christ. My goal was to be a "fisher of men" like Jesus spoke about (Luke 5:10). There was a burning in my heart to share Christ, and I was sure that they could have their lives changed just as I had experienced.

Most weeks I could be found at a little smoke-filled café not too far from my home. I did not always attempt to witness to the rough group of men gathered there early in the morning. Instead I would just sit in and listen to their stories and talk with them about things in general. My hope was that they would see that I cared about them and did not think that I was too good to associate with them. Sometimes I had an opportunity to witness and sometimes I did not. Either way, I kept fishing.

One day, I got up early and headed down to a place which was back in a wooded area off the beaten path where most respectable folks would never go. I would have never gone there again if I did not believe that the Lord wanted me to go. The place to which I was headed was merely called the "barn." What it was in reality was a place where people would gather on the weekends to drink, do drugs, and gamble. I was familiar with it because of my past "activities." All types of people would be there — both men and women. Most were just looking for a good time, but there were also some extremely mean people that frequented the place. That is one reason that it was not the wisest place to go. Even the sheriff's department and other agencies thought twice about that place.

Just the same I decided that the "barn" was the place that the Lord wanted me to go that morning. When I arrived and went in, I found people passed out all over the place from the partying of the night before. Seeing a guy I knew, I roused him awake. "Y'all get up!" I said. "I want to talk to you." The guy roused up and looked at me through bleary eyes, a bit surprised. "Wade, are you crazy? What are you doing here?"

"I want to tell all of you about what the Lord has done in my life." Our conversation continued to rouse people in the place. Before long, men and women were coming out of rooms from all over. It was the strangest thing. They just came into where I was and began sitting down. As I began to share what the Lord had done for me, though grown and devoted to a wild lifestyle, every one of them sat there like little children and listened to what I had to say. I told them of all that the Lord had done for me and that He loved them and that He would do the same for them if they would let him.

When I finished, many had tears running down their cheeks and came up and hugged me and thanked me for caring enough to come and tell them what I had. No one wanted to pray then, so I turned and left. Still, I did receive a phone call that evening from one of the guys there. He told me, "Wade, you've ruined my day! All I can think about is Jesus. I can't even gamble for Him being on my mind."

Later that night, I heard a knock on my door. When I opened it, there stood one of the roughest men I knew. He had been at the barn that morning. His eyes were past being bloodshot from all the drugs and alcohol he had been consuming. They were so red almost no white could be seen at all. As he stood before me, he asked, "Would Jesus really do the same for me that he has done for you?" I assured him that He would. "Would he do it for me tonight?" I said that He would and He did. Our pastor came over and we prayed with him until he knew that he had been changed. Later as he looked into a mirror on the wall, we heard him say, "Look at me! Look at me! Even my eyes have cleared up. All the red is gone!" You can believe it or not, but the red was gone from his eyes and they were as white as a normal person's eyes would be.

An Unofficial Chaplain

I had been working wherever I could when, through a friend and the grace of God, I had the opportunity to get a really good job with the Tennessee Valley Authority (TVA). Once with TVA, not only did I see the opportunity for a great career, I also saw 50,000 employees to whom I could minister the grace and message of my Lord Jesus Christ. I knew that I could not reach them all, but I knew that I could reach some. God had shown me that the only way that I could really make my life count the way I wanted to was to do it through Him. I realize that some would find fault with the idea of someone sharing his faith in the workplace, yet I found countless numbers of people over the years—many without a church or pastor—who needed to hear an encouraging message, needed someone to pray with them, or needed ministry of some type for their families. Besides, no one makes an issue of all the other "talk" that is unrelated to the workplace and often of an unsavory nature.

My prayer became, "Lord, would you allow me to be the unofficial chaplain of TVA? No one will have to know about it but you and me." Consequently, unknown to others, the TVA became my congregation. I always did my job at TVA first, but when the opportunity presented itself, I did my job for the Lord. My goal was not to get them to come to my church or even believe everything like I did. My goal was simply to share the powerful healing message of Jesus Christ to people who might never walk through church doors to hear it.

Over 31 years I saw God do great things in the lives of the people I encountered on the job. I have seen multiple people accept Christ on the job, which in turn, gave them peace and may have helped them in their jobs as well as in their lives. I have prayed for those who were sick and gone to their homes when requested and ministered to their families. I have been asked to give spiritual counsel and even to perform weddings. It would be difficult to call to remembrance all the great people with whom I have worked over the years at TVA.

CHAPTER 10

Old Wounds
Begin to Heal

—————

My life had really taken shape in the years since I was reunited with Gail and had given my life to Jesus Christ. I had a beautiful family, a good job, and the Lord had been giving me opportunities to witness and minister for Him—both in church and out. Many times over the years I had wondered about the men with whom I served in Vietnam. I wondered what had happened to them, where they were living, and how their lives had turned out after the war. Yet, I had never prayed about or even talked about finding them. I guess that it was just something with which I had not allowed myself to become obsessed. Maybe I would find them someday.

As far as staying in contact with the guys with whom I served, it had been almost impossible. The Vietnam era was not a time of modern communications and information systems as it is today. There was no Internet. There were few ways of tracking people. We never thought much about collecting addresses for when we got home. Many of us lost touch and we never saw one another again. We usually did not think that far in advance. All we thought about in the field was surviving.

It was 1994 and I was speaking at a small church's revival at night and working all day. As I came in the house tired from work one afternoon, I noticed a letter on the kitchen counter. The unopened envelop bore the 101st Airborne insignia. Stopping in my tracks, I looked at Gail and said, "The Lord has done something for me, hasn't He?" "I think so," she replied. When I opened the letter there were the names, addresses, and phone numbers of almost every member of the 101st with whom I had served in Vietnam. Someone had prepared the list and had sent it out to all the members of the 101st on the list.

Looking down the list, I found their names one by one. Dave Testerman, Don Stewart, the list went on and on, but one name was missing—Douglas Wineglass. The last time I saw Wineglass was in May 1969. *What could have happened to him?*

I wondered. I really wanted to find him, but I had no idea of how to do it.

Nevertheless, I was excited to have found the men on the list. I remember calling Sergent Dave Testerman. His wife answered the phone and I told her who I was and asked to speak to him. She said that he was out, but for me not to leave my house; he would be back shortly and would want to call me. She said that she knew my name because she had heard of him speak of me often. When he did call, it was a great day, and he told me he was coming to Alabama to see me. We got together that December for a long awaited and anticipated reunion.

A couple of years went by after I received the letter, and my son-in-law at that time was in the Army Reserves. After graduating from basic training in Fort Leonard Wood, Missouri he went on to a base in Virginia. He had been there two or three weeks when he called me one day and told me that he noticed the name tag on another soldier's uniform read "Wineglass." Having heard my testimonies and stories of Vietnam, he asked, "You think it could be his son?" "Will you see him again?" I asked. He said that he would so I told him to ask if his father served in the 101st in Vietnam.

I waited for his call the next day, and sure enough when he called, he said, "It's him! It's him! I've got his phone number!"

When I called, his daughter answered and then went to get her father. Once he was on the phone, I asked, "Do you have any idea who this is?" "No, I don't," he replied. "Do you remember Franks?" I asked. With that he dropped the phone and I could hear him yelling! When he picked up the phone again, I knew that he was as happy as I was that we had found one another. However, the blessing got better when I asked him what he did for a living. He said, "I preach the gospel of the Lord Jesus Christ!"

That's how the Lord found Wineglass for me.

Part of the healing that God has provided for me was the opportunity to find closure on past events through various means. One such opportunity was in the form of a visit to see the parents of Craig Simeone from Cohasset, Massachusetts. Craig had died at Hamburger Hill beside Robert Watt from Humble, Texas.

During all those years I had spent drunk or high, I always wanted to reconnect with the guys I fought beside in Vietnam. The memories have remained fresh over the years and were especially so in those early days of being back home. I had tried reaching anyone I could find, even the parents of these men, but no matter how hard I tried, it just never seemed to work.

Any thoughts of finding the men from my squad had been put aside for years prior to receiving the letter with the names and addresses of the members of the 101st. Finding those guys was great. Still, there was more that God had in store for me that would continue the healing. It was just a few weeks before 9/11 and I had been a Christian at that point for many years. On that day things seemed different. There is no other way to explain it other than to say that I felt that the Holy Spirit was prompting me to make a phone call. Though not audible, it seemed that I could hear the Holy Spirit say to me, "Dial the operator and you will find Craig Simeone's parents today." It was an unusual prompting because I had not been thinking of trying to contact Craig's parents.

It was such a strong urging of the Spirit that I soon found myself dialing the operator. When the operator answered, I told him what I was doing and asked if he could help me find Craig's father. At that time, I did not even know what town he was from, but the operator assured me with a tone of determination in his voice, "If his parents are still alive, you will find them today." After a brief time the operator told me that he had found a Lou Simeone. From what I could remember from hearing Craig talk about his parents, I believed there was a good chance it would be him. "I will stay on the line until you find out if this is him," the operator informed me just before he made the connection.

The phone began ringing and soon there was the voice of an elderly man on the other end. "I'm Wade Franks from Alabama," I started. "Do you have a son by the name of Craig Simeone?" I asked. "This is not a prank, is it?" the man replied. I assured him that it was not. "Well, I did have a son," he began, "but he died in May of 1969 in Vietnam." I began to weep. "I'm so sorry that it took me so many years, but I was with your son when he died in Vietnam."

What I said shook him a bit, but he quickly responded, "Please don't hang up! My wife, June, is at the school and she will be back shortly. I want you to tell her what you have just told me." I told him that I would have to hang up just then, but I promised to call him back that evening when she would be home.

When I did call them back that evening, they were both astonished and grateful that I had called and wanted to know more about what had happened to their son. The Army had only told them that he had been killed in the Thua Thien province of Vietnam. "Please come to see us soon!" they invited. Having just returned from another trip to Vietnam, I was short on money for traveling, so I told them that I would as soon as I could. "Would you hurry?" Mr. Simeone asked. His kidneys had failed and he was on dialysis. His health was fading quickly. I badly wanted to make the trip, but how?

Gail and I began to pray, and that following weekend was when our church had scheduled Dave Roever to be in service with us. When his bus arrived, I went out to meet him. Once on the bus and in conversation, I began to tell him about finding Craig's parents and that they wanted desperately for me to come see them as soon as possible. "Well, can you go?" Dave asked. "Yeah, I'm going just as soon as I get the chance and the extra money," I told him. "No. You're going now!" Dave scolded me. "This is a divine appointment. God arranged this!" Dave told me firmly to call his office the next morning, and his office would arrange the trip for me.

It was only a short time and we were on our way to Cohasset, Massachusetts. Arriving at the airport, we found that Craig's parents were there to meet us. I saw firsthand how sick Craig's dad was and understood the urgency in his invitation when I saw his wife holding him up as he walked through the airport. In the coming days, we would find that being with the Simeones, Lou and June, was like being with old friends. It was as if we had always known them. We sat around their dining room table and shared photos and memories. They took us to see the memorial for Craig and the street named after him.

They had known nothing of the events surrounding the death of their son. It made us wonder how many times they had thought about their son and wondered what had happened to him. Little by little I told them of his last days with me—how we shared the contents of the care package that his mother June had sent—and how we laughed and shared stories from home. We had not just shared the food in the box; we had shared in the love she had sent to her son. Then I told them of that rainy night on Hamburger Hill when our squad had been overrun by the NVA. It seemed that it meant a good bit to his dad that Craig had died in the heat of battle defending his friends and not in an accident of some kind.

In the end, it was a great weekend. It was as good for them as it was for me that I had made the trip. For them it seemed like getting another piece of their son back. It was one last act of friendship for my friend who never made it home alive to tell his story. For me it was one more opportunity to make my life count.

CHAPTER 11

Meeting Dave

B efore I continue with my story, I need to stop and digress for a moment to relate the events of how I met Dave Roever and began working with his ministry. Dave Roever is an important part of my story because it was meeting Dave that started everything in motion to make a return trip to Vietnam possible. And it was returning to Vietnam as a guest of his ministry that God used to bring unfathomable healing into my life.

Unexpectedly, I found myself at a point in my life where I had started finding friends and making connections. For all the years since Vietnam, I had been haunted by memories of the events of that war—events like the time I was unable to pull Watt and others like Sergeant Dotter down that ridge on Hamburger Hill to safety. In my mind I knew it had been impossible to reach them, yet the reality of it was almost too difficult to accept. I could not get to them in time either. There was so much I had been powerless to change; perhaps that was why those memories had haunted me for so long.

Even though I had been awarded three bronze stars, two purple hearts, the Air Medal and several Vietnam Campaign ribbons, and I had done my best in Vietnam as a soldier, I have felt unworthy to talk about what happened because the real heroes died there. Other times I would think when my life was over, perhaps the guys I lost might ask, "Wade, what did you do with your life?" That is why I want my life to count.

I remember that I was visiting the Livingston Chapel United Methodist Church in Crane Hill, Alabama, when a friend of mine from the job (we call him "Bucket") told me about Dave Roever's selecting a number of Christian Vietnam veterans to return with him to Vietnam in 1998. "Would you be interested?" he asked. "How would I go?" was my response. Bucket just persisted, "Tell me, would you go?" "Well, yeah, I would go," I said. He went on to inform me that his church would help me go if I were selected. Although I doubted my chances were good that I would be selected, I got in touch with Dave's ministry and filled out the applications. His office contacted me a few weeks afterward and told me that I had been accepted.

It was on that trip that I would meet Dave Roever. Now, I go back every year and sometimes twice a year. I have been all over Vietnam, but it all began with God's placing Dave Roever in my life.

I first saw Dave at a Camp Meeting service in Birmingham, Alabama. A friend had invited me to go and hear him speak. I had heard speakers before who were Vietnam vets, but their stories seemed to ring hollow or seemed unbelievable or inaccurate to someone who had been in the "trenches." Not knowing Dave at that time, I was skeptical but willing to listen to what he had to say.

I had heard a little about his testimony, but had never heard him speak in person. Dave had been horribly burned over a large portion of his body by the explosion of a phosphorous grenade while serving in Vietnam. His recovery, life, and ministry afterward is a testimony to the miraculous grace and power of God. Dave now has a world-wide ministry, but perhaps is best known to some for speaking in high schools and churches around the country in addition to being a featured speaker at Promise Keepers and on TBN.

Once I heard him, I could see that, not only was he the real deal, but also I sensed that he really cared. There was an anointing upon his ministry that was undeniable. At the end of the service, he had the Vietnam veterans come down front. It was the first time anything like that had happened to me. Even then I felt unworthy to walk down front, but I went anyway. Dave did what he did in a way that made it clear that he meant what he was saying. He really wanted to do that for the veterans. It was a memorable night and the beginning of a new work of God being done in my life.

I did not hear of him again until 1997. At that point in my life, I had begun going to churches and schools and speaking about my experiences in Vietnam and the difference that Jesus Christ had made in my life. It was also at that point that I had my first opportunity to return to Vietnam as a participant of Dave's ministry.

I could never forget the first thing Dave told us on that first trip. He said, "All of you have been handpicked by the Almighty for this journey. I also want you to know that this is not a Dave Roever thing, it is not an American thing; this is truly a God thing! This work is so much bigger than any of us." As I sat there in the chapel service where Dave was speaking, I began to cry. The others thought that I was just emotionally upset—overwhelmed by being back in Vietnam. This was not the case. I was crying out of joy! The Lord had arranged this! I was so happy just to be a part of that journey. I did not know what it would be like in the days ahead, but I knew God had arranged this for me.

Dave Roever is a man who is central to my healing for so many reasons. In spite of all the things I had thought about, the nightmares I had endured, the memories of the battles, I have been able to find closure—in part—to this one man's obedience. As I listened to him that day and on many other instances, it struck me that Dave had not treated me or anyone else I had ever known as if he were better than we were. In fact, he treated everyone as though they are more important than he is. He is a genuinely kind, gentle, and humble man— he's sort of like Jesus!

For many years now, Dave Roever has championed the cause of veterans and young people and children around the world. I believe in what he is doing in Vietnam and all over the world.

I left part of myself in Vietnam when I came home in 1970. My healing is really tied, in part, to Jesus giving me a real friend—not because of what he can do for me—but because God put him in my life. God had a man. He was the right person at the right time. He was a person who I could trust and who would listen. God placed Dave in my life at the right time because He knew that he was the man who could lead me into the completion of the healing God had for me. Dave has led me and many others over the hill into the complete healing that awaited each of us. He will never be able to count, this side of heaven, all the healings that have taken place in my life and in the lives of others. I know it is a God thing! Yet, I can't ignore the fact that God used Dave Roever as His instrument when He was doing His work in my life.

CHAPTER 12

The
Journey Back

———

Making a journey back to Vietnam, a place that I feared I would never leave, and a place where I saw so much death and destruction, might seem like an odd thing for me to do. However, this time I went to Vietnam with a new purpose and with the knowledge that God was doing a new work in my life that had everything to do with giving life and hope to others. Although I never knew them, I always longed to touch the lives of the people of Vietnam. I remember sitting in bars drinking and watching the news reports about politicians going back over to Vietnam, and I would think, *I would like to go back over there one day.* So many significant moments and experiences that shaped my life and my thinking happened there, and so many of my friends had died there. There was just a connection that I could not help but feel.

Trips for veterans back to the battlefields of their youth are becoming more and more popular. Maybe it is the reliving of the past. Maybe they too seek to have old wounds healed. Perhaps they too just want to remember friends whose lives are worth remembering. Everyone has his own purpose.

I knew that I would not be going back because of my "connections" or because of being in a place of influence. I would return because God arranged it. It was a "God thing" as we say around my house. Anything that I can testify about concerning surviving Vietnam or being able to return to Vietnam is strictly God and only God. Everyone that I have met, every contact, every experience, is something God did. He gets all the glory! God would tell me, "Pay attention! That is the only way you can see what is being given back to you." He constantly reminds me, "I will restore!"

Going back to Vietnam is not for everyone. There needs to be a spiritual connection for it to really benefit the person. Some vets are still bitter about what they experienced in the past or else they simply have no interest in revisiting. However, for the Vietnam veteran who is looking for peace, reconciliation, and closure, it can be a life-changing journey. Attitude plays a major role.

When I returned, I felt close to the friends that I lost over there. I may want to forget the trauma of the war, but I never want to forget those guys that shared one of the most transformative times of my life. I go back to complete the healing process in my life and to help begin, or be a part of, the healing in the lives of other veterans who return. I go because God sends me.

I have been back to the A Shau Valley and stood in a village not two miles from Hamburger Hill and was able to see that infamous hill where friends gave their all. Across the valley there was Eagle's Nest, where we waited for the call to come to Hamburger Hill. I've been back to LZ Sally, where I had buried Little Joe, and numerous other places.

On the other hand, old battlefields are not my primary destination. My reasons have become bigger than the war and the past. Now my reasons for returning are centered on the continuing effort to make my life count and to fulfill my purpose in life. Now I make the trip not to relive past deaths and tragedies but to impart life and hope to a new generation of Vietnamese people. Furthermore, I return to see and be a part of what God is doing in Vietnam. I go to help the children, to support the medical missions, the ministries and the orphanages. I go to support the Christian people who are laying their lives on the line for the gospel of Jesus Christ everyday. I go back to help widen the door that is opening that will one day lead to the freedom to take the gospel to all the people of Vietnam, without the control or censorship of the communist government.

No, I never get to stand on a stage and preach a crusade before thousands of people. It's not about that. It's not about being in the spotlight. It is about being a part of what God is doing through so many people. I, and others, participate in this mission through an organization called Roever Educational Assistance Programs (REAP).

We do all we can to take the gospel everywhere we go. No, the communist government will not allow us to hold crusades. But we preach the gospel through encouragement to other Christians and through water wells dug for remote villages so that little children will not die or be sick from waterborne illnesses. We preach Jesus through providing free medical care for the poorest of Vietnam, through scholarships for children to attend school, through giving bicycles to rural pastors to help them carry the gospel. We preach with paint brushes and repair work on orphanages. We preach by going to orphanages bearing gifts, playing games with the children and sitting and eating from the same loaf of bread broken by the little hands of children who have nothing else to give. But they share all that they have with a smile and a hug. Of course, we preach. Sometimes we even use words.

CHAPTER 13

From the Poncho to the Palace

―――

It was 2001 and my seventh trip back to Vietnam. On this trip, we were venturing northeast of Saigon to a place called Na Trang. Gail was with me on this trip, which made it even more special. There was so much that I wanted to share with her about Vietnam that she could only experience by being there. In fact, I believe that God planned it that way because He wanted Gail to share in what He was going to do for me on this trip.

Things had not been as interesting as they had on previous trips, and I was wondering and watching to see if God was going to do something special. He had always seemed to provide a spiritual dimension to previous trips, and I was hungry to experience something new in my healing. We rode along on the bus up a winding road to high up in the mountains—one of the highest points in Vietnam. We were so high up that the usual hot, humid air had now grown cool and crisp.

Nearing the top of the mountain, the bus slowed and we found ourselves pulling up to a place with huge gates hung on grand stone placements. Behind the gates we could see a white palace with perfectly manicured lawns and gardens that would rival or surpass those of the gardens and golf course in Augusta, Georgia. We often visit historical sights along the way as we travel through Vietnam, but we had never seen anything like this. It had been built by the French when they colonized Vietnam many years before. It was used as a place of rest and relaxation for high-ranking French officers. The sign read, "Dalot Palace."

Those in charge of our group had gotten off the bus and were talking to the guards. "Wow! Are we going to stay here?" Gail asked in awe of its beauty. "I don't know," I replied as I stared out the window. That would be too good to be true. But as a procession of uniform clad workers headed toward our bus and opened the luggage storage compartment, it became apparent that we were.

The moment that I stepped off the bus I knew that this was the place where God was going to do something special. As I walked toward the palace, thoughts of the events of 1969 began flooding my mind. The faces and memories of the men with whom I served like Watt, Sgt. Testerman, Captain Franzinger, Wineglass, Sig, Stewart and Craig Simeone came before me as though it were yesterday. The terrible things I had experienced came storming through my mind.

My thoughts were temporarily interrupted when they came for us. "Mr. Franks, come with me please." Gail and I walked up the stairs and down a hallway. We stopped in front of another large interior door. We were led through the doorway into a small foyer and then through another door. We walked into what would be our room. The floors were made of beautiful hardwood. The bed looked to be made of mahogany topped with a canopy, and the canopy was covered with a sheer material. The bathtub sat up on pedestal legs and the water literally ran a pale blue from the tap. The room and all its furnishings were obviously from a previous time period. The room itself was a snapshot in time.

Wade and Gail Franks on the grounds of Dalot Palace

Gail and I were both astonished at the beauty of the palace and suite we were given. Never before and never since have we stayed at such a place. But we were there for a reason. I could sense that God had something to reveal to me. I was still speechless, caught up in the moment, and overwhelmed by the sensation of God's presence. I could hear Gail in the background describing everything she saw throughout the suite and asking me what I had done with the camera.

To my right I saw two of the largest French doors I had ever seen that led outside, so I opened them to see what kind of view we had from our room. In order to step through, I had to open two large outer shutters. The shutters opened up to reveal a large balcony. The cool mountain breeze flooded past me into the room, causing the sheer canopy drapes to flutter in the flowing breeze.

Once out onto the balcony, I saw before me the lushest green mountainside that I had ever seen. Trying hard to take in all the beauty of the scenery, the words came so clearly to my mind from the Holy Spirit. Although I was all alone, it was as real as if a man stood beside me and spoke. I knew that it was the Lord speaking to me. He said, "Over thirty years ago you were sleeping under a poncho in a mud hole, but today I have brought you from that poncho to this palace in a country where so much had been taken from you. Today, I am giving back to you so many things that you have lost."

If God has taught me anything in the last number of years, He has taught me to pay attention! Many times I have heard the voice of the Holy Spirit remind me to "pay attention," and I would see what God was doing in my life to heal me and to restore what had been lost.

As I stood on that balcony of Dalot Palace and looked out over the valley and rolling mountains before me, I finally saw with great clarity what had been happening— what God had been doing those thirty years. My journey that began in the mud of the Vietnam jungle, where I lay under a canopy made from my poncho and thought I would surely die and be forgotten, had come full circle in the very country where I had lost part of my life and my heart. God had never forgotten me.

I have always wanted my life to count—especially since Vietnam. It is a debt that I feel I owe to those men who never came home. I did not deserve to come home when they did not. Call it survivor's guilt or whatever you want to call it, but I still feel that I owe them. I was given an opportunity they were not. But many years ago, because of the Lord, I decided then that I would not allow a dark past to ruin a bright future.

Obviously, Vietnam has had a tremendous impact upon my life and a hand in shaping me into the man that I am today, but it was God's hand that has molded and shaped me most. I am not ashamed of either. It was God's hand that reached down in the jungles of Vietnam and held me firmly in His grasp lest more than my life be lost.

Nevertheless, telling the stories or revealing information about medals awarded or about accomplishments as a part of this book or as a part of speaking at veteran's services is often difficult simply because I survived. Better men than I did not. In some way I feel guilty for receiving any honor for serving my country. Many more deserving men were never awarded the medals and citations that they deserved simply because their heroic deeds were witnessed by too few or by none at all but God. Yet, they were there and gave their all.

I do what I do, in part, to draw attention to these men and to what Jesus Christ has done in my life to heal me and to restore what was lost in previous years. My story is not about "guts and glory" on the battlefield. Nor is it about how low drugs and alcohol can take a man. My story is about wounds that have been healed. It is about honoring my friends and about honoring my Savior Who has brought me out of despair, Who bound up my wounds, Who poured His healing oil into my soul and Who brought my life full circle and allowed me to see the work of His hands in a way I had never seen before.

He has given me the desires of my heart and the refreshing of my soul. Now the place I never thought I would leave alive is the place I return to in order to share the healing and the hope of the Savior I serve with the people who are my friends and the object of my compassion. The hopelessness and fear of past days are behind me now and what lies ahead are, no doubt, the greatest days of God's glory revealed in my life.

Printed in the United States
104584LV00001B/1-312/A